THE QUOTABLE

DOUCHEBAG

THE QUOTABLE
DOUCHEBAG

A TREASURY OF SPECTACULARLY STUPID REMARKS

COMPILED BY
**MARGARET
McGUIRE**

QUIRK BOOKS
PHILADELPHIA

Library of Congress Cataloging in Publication Number: 2009923855

ISBN: 978-1-59474-425-9

Printed in China

Typeset in Futura

Designed by Doogie Horner
Production management by John J. McGurk

Cover photography by Jimi Robinson
Interior photography courtesy of the Everett Collection

Distributed in North America by Chronicle Books
680 Second Street
San Francisco, CA 94107

10 9 8 7 6 5 4 3 2

Quirk Books
215 Church Street
Philadelphia, PA 19106
www.irreference.com
www.quirkbooks.com

WHAT MAKES A MAN A DOUCHEBAG?

To answer this question, we must look to the annals of history. The first douchebags were manufactured in the 1920s by American companies such as Lysol, Fresca, Sterizol, and Zonite. Their product derived its name from the French *la douche*, meaning "to shower," and it was first marketed as a cleansing cure for lonely, malodorous spinsterhood.

Ironically, these early douchebags failed to work as promised. Instead of preventing so-called "not so fresh" feelings, douchebags actually caused them. By the end of the twentieth century, health experts warned women that douching increases the risk of bacterial infections, pelvic inflammation, sterility, ectopic pregnancy, and sexually transmitted diseases.

Which helps explain why now, at the start of the twenty-first century, we bestow the name of this much-disparaged product upon so many different men—everyone from actors and athletes to musicians and world leaders. John Mayer is a douchebag. All Fox News anchors are douchebags.

Suddenly, it seems, the world is full of douchebags.

The Quotable Douchebag is more than a compilation of their most inappropriate remarks. It is designed to serve as an educational primer—a means for illustrating their arrogance, vanity, machismo, and cluelessness. Should you encounter a man with similar traits, run.

The feathered [hair] cut projects an attitude of ease and quiet confidence that seems to have all but eluded our generation. This is a work in progress, and as my hair grows longer it will serve to become a more stirring and poignant statement.

—John Mayer, American musician (1977–), on his '80s haircut

[MY HAIR] CREATES THIS TARZANESQUE, LIKABLE BAD-BOY IMAGE. IT SAYS,

"I AM A WILD CHILD. I WILL TAKE YOU ON A HARLEY RIDE, THEN MAKE PASSIONATE LOVE TO YOU. AND SHOULD YOU BE ATTACKED BY A LION OR AN IDIOT AT A BAR, I WILL PROTECT YOU."

—Bret Michaels (1963–), American singer and reality TV personality

I'M A T-SHIRT GUY NOW. BUT WIFEBEATERS WON'T GO OUT OF STYLE, NOT AS LONG AS BITCHES KEEP MOUTHING OFF.

—Marshall Mathers III, a.k.a. Eminem (1972–), American rapper

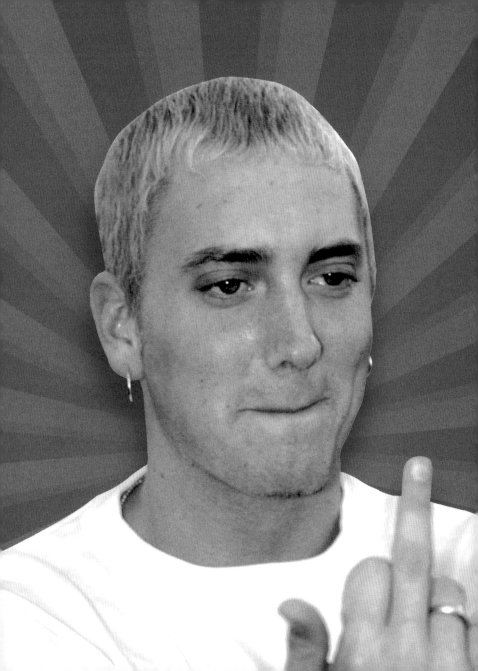

Of course you have me in my underwear in front of high-level employees. Guess what? I design underwear!

—Dov Charney, CEO of American Apparel (1969–), responding to allegations that he walked around the office wearing nothing but underpants

That's a wonderful side effect of leather pants: When you pee yourself in them, they're more forgiving than jeans.

—Slash (1965–), English rock star

MY SKIN IS MORE BEAUTIFUL THAN YOURS.

I WOULD BE QUITE MORE POPULAR IN JAIL IF I SO CHOSE.

—Gene Simmons (1949–), Israeli-American rock star, to NPR talk show host Terry Gross

THE DOUCHEBAG HALL OF FAME:

David Hasselhoff

(1952–), AMERICAN ACTOR

I believe the camera photographs your aura, and it also photographs your heart. And I cast *Baywatch* that way. I wanted to play around with the format, really tear it to pieces and shake it up. For example, if Mitch saves someone from drowning, and that person then goes out and releases a virus that kills a million people. Imagine the moral implications of that.

THERE ARE MANY DYING CHILDREN OUT THERE WHOSE LAST WISH IS TO MEET ME.

I'M MORE GHETTO, AND BALLROOM IS MORE VANILLA. I'VE HAD TO LEARN HOW TO BE VANILLA.

—Lance Bass (1979–), American pop star and member of N*Sync, on coming to terms with his innate "ghetto" dance style

I KNOW WHO I AM.
NO ONE ELSE KNOWS WHO I AM. IF I WAS A GIRAFFE AND SOMEBODY SAID I WAS A SNAKE, I'D THINK, "NO, ACTUALLY I AM A GIRAFFE."

—Richard Gere (1949–), American actor

I THINK

THE JEWS

NEED ME

RIGHT NOW.

—Geraldo Rivera (1943–), American journalist and talk show host,
describing his decision to embrace his Jewish heritage

BAD WEATHER IS LIKE RAPE. IF IT'S INEVITABLE, JUST RELAX AND ENJOY IT.

—Clayton Williams (1931–), Republican candidate for governor of Texas in 1990

I BELIEVE IN JESUS CHRIST, AND IF YOU DON'T THAT'S OKAY, BECAUSE YOU'RE GONNA FRY LIKE A JIMMY DEAN PURE PORK SAUSAGE.

—Ken Hutcherson (1952–), American pastor of the Antioch Bible Church and NFL linebacker

I'M THE MAN! . . . I SAY THAT 'CAUSE I MAKE A MILLION BUCKS. I AM A GOD, I HAVE AN AGENT, AND, OH, I AM THE GUNS [FLEXES MUSCLES].

—Danny Bonaduce (1959–), American TV personality and former child actor

I've said [I make] a million dollars. That's not actually accurate. I make—I am as famous as I can bear being.

—Danny Bonaduce (1959–), American TV personality and former child actor

I AM A THING OF BEAUTY.

—Frank Sinatra (1915–1998), American singer and actor

I find myself fascinating.

—Milan Kundera (1929–), Czech and French novelist

I HAVE SIGNED THOUSANDS OF BREASTS.

—Dane Cook (1972–), American stand-up comedian

Every morning when I wake up, I experience an exquisite joy—the joy of being Salvador Dalí—and I ask myself in rapture: What wonderful things this Salvador Dalí is going to accomplish today?

—Salvador Dalí (1904–1989), Spanish painter

PEOPLE HATE ME BECAUSE I AM A **MULTIFACETED, TALENTED, WEALTHY, INTERNATIONALLY FAMOUS GENIUS.**

—Jerry Lewis (1926–), American comedian

I SEE MY BODY AS A

CLASSY CHASSIS

TO CARRY MY MIND AROUND IN.

—Sylvester Stallone (1946–), American actor, director, and producer

I LIKE
THE MOMENT WHEN

I BREAK A
MAN'S EGO.

—Bobby Fischer, American chess grandmaster (1943–2008)

I'm aware, as a sane person, that I'm not the best-looking guy in the world. I'm aware of it. But when I go into a party, I will walk out with your girlfriend.

—Gene Simmons (1949–), Israeli-American rock star

I stopped painting in 1990 at the peak of my success just to deny people my beautiful paintings; and I did it out of spite.

—Vincent Gallo (1961–), Italian-American actor, director, and producer

ALL MEN SHALL BE MY SLAVES! ALL WOMEN SHALL SUCCUMB TO MY CHARMS! ALL MANKIND SHALL GROVEL AT MY FEET AND NOT KNOW WHY!

—L. Ron Hubbard (1911–1986), American sci-fi novelist and founder of Scientology, as quoted by former Scientologist Margery Wakefield

THE DOUCHEBAG HALL OF FAME:

Mike Tyson

(1966–), AMERICAN PUGILIST

I normally don't do interviews with women unless I fornicate with them. So you shouldn't talk any more, unless you want to, you know.

I'M ON THE ZOLOFT THING, RIGHT? BUT I'M ON THAT TO KEEP ME FROM KILLING Y'ALL!

You guys can't define me or define my work as a father. I am many things, you know. I am many things, yeah, I am a convicted rapist, I'm a hell raiser, I'm a father—a loving father, I'm a semi-good husband, you know what I mean.

THESE ARE THE PRETTIEST WITNESSES WE HAVE HAD IN A LONG TIME. I IMAGINE YOU ARE ALL MARRIED. IF NOT, YOU COULD BE IF YOU WANTED TO BE.

—Strom Thurmond (1902–2003), Republican senator from South Carolina, to a group of feminists testifying before the Senate

I've had to overcome a lot of diversity.

—Drew Gooden (1981–), American professional basketball player

NOW TELL ME THE TRUTH BOYS, IS THIS KIND OF FUN?

—Tom DeLay (1947–), Republican representative from Texas and House majority leader, to three young Hurricane Katrina evacuees at the Astrodome in Houston in 2005

THE HOLOCAUST WAS AN OBSCENE PERIOD IN OUR NATION'S HISTORY. I MEAN IN THIS CENTURY'S HISTORY. BUT WE ALL LIVED IN THIS CENTURY. I DIDN'T LIVE IN THIS CENTURY.

—Dan Quayle (1947–), vice president of the United States

When a great many people are unable to find work, unemployment results.

—Calvin Coolidge (1872–1933), president of the United States

A few years ago, everybody was saying, "We must have more leisure, everybody's working too much." Now that everybody's got more leisure, they're complaining they're unemployed. People don't seem to be able to make up their minds what they want, do they?

—Prince Philip (1921–), English consort of Queen Elizabeth II, when asked for his thoughts on unemployment in Britain during a severe economic recession in 1981

THE MORE WE REMOVE PENALTIES FOR BEING A BUM, THE MORE BUMISM IS GOING TO BLOSSOM.

—Jesse Helms (1921–2008), Republican senator from North Carolina, arguing his case against welfare

The picture in the paper is of Kurt Cobain in a pair of ragged jeans with a hole in the knee. I doubt that Kurt Cobain ever prayed or did the kind of work that would have worn a hole in his pants.

—Andy Rooney, American radio and TV writer (1919–), on the picture of Kurt Cobain in his obituary

The poor homosexuals, they have declared war upon nature, and now nature is extracting awful retribution.

—Pat Buchanan (1938–), American conservative political commentator, discussing AIDS in 1983

FACTS ARE STUPID THINGS.

—Ronald Reagan (1911–2004), president of the United States, paraphrasing John Adams's quotation "Facts are stubborn things" at the 1988 Republican National Convention

I've never seen a man in my life I wanted to marry. And I'm going to be blunt and plain: If one ever looks at me like that, I'm going to kill him and tell God he died.

—Jimmy Swaggart (1935–), American Pentecostal preacher and televangelist

Some people think that our planet is suffering from a fever. Now scientists are telling us that Mars is experiencing its own planetary warming: Martian warming.

—Fred Thompson (1942–), Republican senator from Tennessee and actor, in an article deriding the idea of global warming

IT'S AN
URBAN LEGEND.
IT NEVER HAPPENED.

—Dick Cheney (1941–), vice president of the United States, on whether or not he expanded vice presidential powers

THE DOUCHEBAG HALL OF FAME:

Liam Gallagher

(1972–), LEAD SINGER OF OASIS

OASIS MIGHT NOT BE THE BIGGEST BAND IN THE WORLD, BUT WE'RE THE BEST.

I respect the Stones but their songs are a pile of crap. As for U2, they don't say a lot or seem like normal persons.

You tell the woman that you want to chill with how much you love her. You bring her flowers. You remember her birthday. You remember your anniversary. You remember her mother's birthday. And then you cheat on her with every possible girl you can.

—Danny Bonaduce (1959–), American TV personality and former child actor, dispensing advice as a life coach for hire on the streets of Hollywood

Canada is a sweet country. It is like your retarded cousin you see at Thanksgiving and sort of pat him on the head. You know, he's nice but you don't take him seriously. That's Canada.

—Tucker Carlson (1969–), American news correspondent and political commentator

I've always thought that underpopulated countries in Africa are vastly under-polluted.

—Lawrence Summers (1954–), American economist and head of the National Economic Council

I went down to [Latin America] to find out from them and [learn] their views. You'd be surprised. They're all individual countries.

—Ronald Reagan (1911–2004), president of the United States

[Vice presidential candidate and Alaska Governor Sarah Palin] does know about foreign relations because she is right up there in Alaska, right next door to Russia.

—Steve Doocy (1956–), American news anchor, on Fox News

I CAN'T REALLY REMEMBER THE NAMES OF THE CLUBS THAT WE WENT TO.

—Shaquille O'Neal (1972–), American professional basketball player, when asked if he visited the **Parthenon** while on a trip to Greece

THE DOUCHEBAG HALL OF FAME:

ROBERT SYLVESTER KELLY, A.K.A.

R. Kelly

(1967–), AMERICAN RAPPER AND R&B SINGER

My greatest competition is, well, me. . . . I'm the Ali of today. I'm the Marvin Gaye of today. I'm the Bob Marley of today. I'm the Martin Luther King, or all the other greats that have come before us. And a lot of people are starting to realize that now.

OSAMA BIN LADEN IS THE ONLY ONE WHO KNOWS EXACTLY WHAT I'M GOING THROUGH.

I love music, and music loves me back. We're kind of married, and I'm pregnant by music.

THE INTERNET IS NOT SOMETHING THAT YOU JUST DUMP SOMETHING ON. IT'S NOT A BIG TRUCK. IT'S A SERIES OF TUBES.

—Ted Stevens (1923–), Republican senator from Alaska and convicted felon,
opposing a net neutrality amendment to his telecommunications bill

SURE, I LOOK LIKE A WHITE MAN. BUT MY HEART IS AS BLACK AS ANYONE'S HERE.

—George Wallace (1919–1998), Democratic governor of Alabama, during his presidential campaign to a mainly black audience

SLAVERY BUILT THE SOUTH.
I'M NOT SAYING WE SHOULD BRING IT BACK; I'M JUST SAYING IT HAD ITS MERITS. FOR ONE THING, THE STREETS WERE SAFER AFTER DARK.

—Rush Limbaugh (1951–), American radio host and political commentator

I COULDN'T IMAGINE SOMEBODY LIKE OSAMA BIN LADEN UNDERSTANDING THE JOY OF HANUKKAH.

—George W. Bush (1946–), president of the United States

MY GOAL IS TO GOAD PEOPLE INTO SAYING SOMETHING THAT RUINS THEIR LIFE.

—Don Imus (1940–), American radio host, describing his daily work as a radio talk show host

THAT'S SOME NAPPY-HEADED HOS THERE.

—Don Imus (1940–), American radio host, describing the Rutger's women's basketball team on April 4, 2008; Imus was fired from his radio show just eight days later.

IF I COULD CHANGE ONE THING ABOUT MYSELF, IT WOULD BE TO LOSE THE

BIMBO ATTRACTOR CHIP

THAT GOD MUST HAVE PLACED IN ME AT BIRTH.

—Kid Rock (1971–), American musician and actor

I don't like any female comedians.
A woman doing comedy doesn't
offend me, but sets me back a bit.
I, as a viewer, have trouble with it.
I think of her as a producing machine
that brings babies in the world.

—Jerry Lewis (1926–), American comedian

Too many good docs are
getting out of the business.
Too many OB-GYNs are
unable to practice their
love with women all across
this country.

—George W. Bush, president of the United States (1946–)

DO YOU KNOW WHY GOD CREATED WOMAN? BECAUSE SHEEP CAN'T TYPE.

—Kenneth Armbrister, Democratic senator from Texas (1946–)

ALL OF THE WOMEN ON *THE APPRENTICE* FLIRTED WITH ME— CONSCIOUSLY OR UNCONSCIOUSLY. THAT'S TO BE EXPECTED.

—Donald Trump (1946–), American mogul

A PRETTY GIRL IS CERTAINLY COMPARABLE TO A GOOD HORSE.

—William Shatner (1931–), American actor

What if your husband woke up one day and announced that he was not in the mood to go to work? If this happened a few times a year, any wife would have sympathy for her hardworking husband. But what if this happened as often as many wives announce that they are not in the mood to have sex? Most women would gradually stop respecting and therefore eventually stop loving such a man.

—Dennis Prager (1948–), American talk show host, ethicist, and public speaker

Women are to have fun with. In politics, I prefer not to see a woman. Instead of getting all worked up, they should stay as they are—like flowers.

—Lech Walesa (1943–), president of Poland

THERE'S NEVER BEEN A WOMAN GRANDMASTER CHESS PLAYER. ONCE YOU GET ONE, THEN I'LL BUY SOME OF THE FEMINISM.

—Pat Robertson (1930–), American televangelist, even though there were five female grandmasters at the time

DO YOU KNOW WHY CHELSEA CLINTON IS SO UGLY? BECAUSE JANET RENO IS HER FATHER.

—John McCain (1936–), Republican senator from Arizona and presidential candidate

THE DOUCHEBAG HALL OF FAME:

Spencer Pratt

(1983–), AMERICAN REALITY TV SHOW PERSONALITY

Madonna, eat your heart out, Britney Spears, eat your heart out. I would say we have diamond records coming— they're gonna sell 10-million plus.

On Mary-Kate Olsen, who discussed Pratt with David Letterman: She should probably focus more on not getting dressed in the dark than on me. . . . I know I've made it in Hollywood when a famous troll is talking about me on *Letterman.* I forgive her, though. She's had to go through life as the less cute twin, which must be tough.

If people aren't hating on you, they don't care, and if they don't care, that means you're not doing anything right.

I'VE NEVER KNOWN A TIME WHEN A **MOTOCROSS RACE** OR A **GREASED PIG CHALLENGE** DIDN'T LEAD TO **TRUE LOVE.**

—Bret Michaels (1963–), American singer and reality TV personality

[I] don't believe there's any difference between a monogamous and a polygamous relationship. Those are all just big words, like *gymnasium.*

—Gene Simmons (1949–), Israeli-American rock star

Why should I limit myself to only one woman when I can have as many women as I want?

—George Gershwin (1898–1937), American composer

I THINK A MAN CAN HAVE TWO, MAYBE THREE AFFAIRS, WHILE HE IS MARRIED. BUT THREE IS THE ABSOLUTE MAXIMUM. AFTER THAT, YOU'RE CHEATING.

—Yves Montand (1921–1991), French actor

I THINK GAY MARRIAGE IS SOMETHING THAT SHOULD BE BETWEEN A MAN AND A WOMAN.

—Arnold Schwarzenegger (1947–), Austrian-American
body builder, actor, and politician

I wanna meet a girl who has nothing to do with L.A., a nice, normal, real girl. Actually, you now, that's gonna be a component of our new MTV show—me leaving L.A. to meet a normal girl. It might be hard, though, with all the cameras.

—Brody Jenner (1983–), American reality TV personality starring in *Princes of Malibu*, *The Hills*, and *Bromance*

I'M THE
HIROSHIMA
OF LOVE.

— Sylvester Stallone (1946–), American actor

MY NOTION OF A WIFE AT FORTY IS THAT A MAN SHOULD BE ABLE TO CHANGE HER, LIKE A BANKNOTE, FOR TWO TWENTIES.

—Warren Beatty (1937–), American actor

SHIT, A FEW YEARS DOWN THE ROAD, AND A COUPLE TOURS LATER, I WOUND UP MEETING HER ASS AGAIN, AND HERE WE ARE [MARRIED].

—Kevin Federline, a.k.a. K-Fed, American dancer, model, and rapper (1978–), discussing Britney Spears

THE DAY YOU TAKE COMPLETE RESPONSIBILITY FOR YOURSELF, THE DAY YOU STOP MAKING ANY EXCUSES, THAT'S THE DAY YOU START TO THE TOP.

—O. J. Simpson (1947–), American football player, actor, and convicted felon

I didn't write it.

—O. J. Simpson (1947–), American football player, actor, and convicted felon, claiming that a ghostwriter was responsible for parts of his 2006 book *If I Did It, Here's How It Happened.*

My fellow astronauts . . .

—Dan Quayle (1947–), vice president of the United States, addressing a crowd on the anniversary of the Apollo 11 mission

I'LL TELL YOU WHO SHOULD BE TORTURED AND KILLED AT GUANTANAMO: EVERY FILTHY DEMOCRAT IN THE U.S. CONGRESS.

—Sean Hannity (1961–), American radio and television host

I love my grandfather, but I just want to slap him across the face for liking FDR—I think that was one evil son of a bitch!

—Glenn Beck (1964–), American radio host

I've been in combat. I've seen it, I've been close to it. And if I'm—my unit is in danger, and I got a captured guy, and the guy knows where the enemy is, and I'm lookin' him in the eye, the guy better tell me. . . . If it's life or death, he's going first.

—Bill O'Reilly (1949–), American political commentator and talk show host, who never actually served in the military

I am convinced that unless America changes course, we will become the France of the 21st century.

—Mitt Romney (1947–), American businessman and governor of Massachusetts, who spent two years in France as a Mormon missionary and is fluent in French

A YEAR FROM NOW, I'LL BE VERY SURPRISED IF THERE IS NOT SOME GRAND SQUARE IN BAGHDAD THAT IS NAMED AFTER PRESIDENT BUSH.

—Richard Perle (1941–), American lobbyist and chairman of a Pentagon advisory board

[Pro-choice men] are either women trapped in men's bodies, like Alan Alda or Phil Donahue, or younger guys who are like camp followers looking for easy sex.

—Bob Dornan (1933–) , Republican representative from California

Why do we assume that it is terribly irresponsible for a man to refuse to go to work because he is not in the mood, but a woman can—indeed, ought to—refuse sex because she is not in the mood? Why?

—Dennis Prager (1948–), American talk show host, ethicist, and public speaker

I would not want to be a politician. . . . If I was campaigning, and I was going against my opponent and he started attacking my character, and I leapt over the table and I choked him unconscious, would that help my campaign?

—Chuck Norris (1940–), American martial artist and actor

I'M SAYING THAT WHEN THE PRESIDENT DOES IT, THAT MEANS THAT IT IS NOT ILLEGAL.

—Richard Nixon (1913–1994), president of the United States

I'D LIKE TO KNOCK SOME GOOD SENSE INTO BARACK [OBAMA]. I WOULDN'T HURT HIM. BUT IF HE WINS THE ELECTION, HE'LL HURT ME.

HE'S A CULTURAL TERRORIST.

—Stephen Baldwin (1966–), American actor, proposing a boxing match between himself and President Barack Obama

I'M THE COMMANDER—

SEE, I DON'T NEED TO EXPLAIN—

I DO NOT NEED TO EXPLAIN WHY I SAY THINGS.

THAT'S THE INTERESTING THING ABOUT BEING PRESIDENT.

—George W. Bush (1946–), president of the United States

If the Supreme Court says that you have the right to consensual [gay] sex within your home, then you have the right to bigamy, you have the right to polygamy, you have the right to incest, you have the right to adultery. You have the right to anything.

—Rick Santorum (1958–), Republican senator from Pennsylvania

I got to be real intimate with people. Going into their living rooms and bedrooms, you know, seeing their underwear.

—Tom DeLay (1947–), Republican representative from Texas and House majority leader, on how his former career as an exterminator prepared him for politics

To be "Orwellian" is to speak with absolute clarity, to be succinct, to explain what the event is, to talk about what triggers something happening. . . . and to do so without any pejorative whatsoever.

—Frank Luntz (1962–), American political commentator, insisting that "Orwellian" is a positive term

LIFE IS VERY IMPORTANT TO AMERICANS.

—Bob Dole (1923–), Republican senator from Kansas

I AM THE FRED ASTAIRE OF KARATE.

—Jean Claude Van Damme (1960–), Belgian martial artist

I cannot tell you how grateful I am. I am filled with humidity.

—Gib Lewis (ca. 1937–), Democratic representative from Texas and Speaker of the House

I HAVEN'T COMMITTED A CRIME. WHAT I DID WAS FAIL TO COMPLY WITH THE LAW.

—David Dinkins (1927–), Democratic mayor of New York City, discussing tax evasion

I'm not indecisive. Am I indecisive?

—Jim Scheibel (1947–), Democratic mayor of St. Paul, Minnesota

I resent your insinuendos.

—Richard Daley (1902–1976), Democratic mayor of Chicago

I've got this thing and it's fucking golden, and, uh, I'm just not giving it up for fuckin' nothing. I'm not gonna do it.

—Rod Blagojevich (1956–), Democratic governor of Illinois, describing his plans to trade or sell President Obama's Senate seat

PAINTINGS ARE LIKE A BEER. ONLY BEER TASTES GOOD, AND IT'S HARD TO STOP DRINKING BEER.

—Billy Carter (1937–1988), American brewer and brother of President Jimmy Carter

LINDA, BECAUSE SHE IS A LADY, IS AFRAID OF MATH.

—George Brown Jr. (1920–1999), Democratic representative from California, responding to his Republican opponent Linda Wilde's plan to eliminate the Department of Education

You know, education, if you make the most of it, you study hard, you do your homework, and you make an effort to be smart, you can do well. If you don't, you get stuck in Iraq.

—John Kerry (1943–), Democratic senator from Massachusetts

THE IDEA THAT YOU CAN DEFEND THIS NATION WITHIN THE CONSTITUTION, UNDER THE LAW, AND TELL THE TRUTH IS STILL CONSIDERED A SORT OF CHILDISH, FEMININE POSITION.

—Walter Mondale (1928–), vice president of the United States

INBREEDING IS HOW WE GET CHAMPIONSHIP HORSES.

—Carl Gunter (1938–1999), Democratic representative from Louisiana, explaining why he opposed a 1990 antiabortion bill that allowed abortion in cases of incest

I am not a chauvinist, obviously. . . . I believe in women's rights for every woman but my own.

—Harold Washington (1922–1987), Democratic mayor of Chicago

YOU MEAN, LIKE A BOOK?

—Justin Timberlake, American entertainer (1981–), in response to a *Rolling Stone* interviewer's question "What was the best thing you've read all year?"

IT'S SEMI-FRUSTRATING WHEN YOUR NAME ACTUALLY BECOMES A

SYNONYM
FOR DOUCHEBAG.

—Pete Wentz (1979–), American musician

I really opened myself up
in [my new film] *JCVD*. I
peeled back the skin of
the fruit, cut the pulp and
then took that very hard
seed. In this film I cut that
hard seed, and inside that
seed was a kind of liquid
cream substance of the
man I am, or the woman
you are. It was like being
naked—I would love to be
naked in front of you.

—Jean Claude Van Damme (1960–), Belgian martial
artist, to *Newsweek*'s Sarah Ball in what was supposed
to be a formal interview

I COULD PULL MY PENIS OUT RIGHT NOW, AND I GUARANTEE YOU NO ONE WOULD BE OFFENDED.

—Dov Charney (1969–), CEO of American Apparel and self-described "Jewish hustler," to the *Jewish Journal* after being served with his first of several sexual harassment suits

I was not drinking. I did not drink either morning. I do not have an alcohol problem. I am not David Hasselhoff. This is not a pattern.

—John Stamos (1963–), American actor, blaming jet lag, sleeping pills, and the Hoff for slurring his speech and making lewd gestures in interviews with Australian news agencies

I'm making a specialty of playing douchebags . . . I could spend the rest of my career perfecting the douchebag.

—Richard Hall, a.k.a. Moby (1965–), American musician, on his acting performances

One of the critics actually called me a douchebag. Which, I am a douchebag, but this guy doesn't fucking know me to call me a douchebag.

—Darren Lynn Bousman (1979–), director of *Saw II*, *Saw III*, and *Saw IV*

SO WE HAD CHENEYS ON BOTH SIDES OF THE FAMILY, AND WE DON'T EVEN LIVE IN WEST VIRGINIA. [CHUCKLES.] YOU CAN SAY THOSE THINGS WHEN YOU'RE NOT RUNNING FOR REELECTION.

—Dick Cheney (1941–), vice president of the United States

IF YOU WANT TO WELCOME ME WITH OPEN ARMS, I'M AFRAID YOU'RE ALSO GOING TO HAVE TO WELCOME ME WITH OPEN LEGS.

—Gene Simmons (1949–), Israeli-American rock star, to NPR talk show host Terry Gross

THE DOUCHEBAG HALL OF FAME:
ROBERT VAN WINKLE, A.K.A.

Vanilla Ice

(1967–), AMERICAN RAPPER

On why "Ice, Ice Baby" does not rip off "Under Pressure" by Queen and David Bowie: You hear that? There's an extra beat at the end. See, it's different.

TIME WILL TELL.
THE ICE MAN IS LEGIT.

On why he'd hired a ghostwriter to pen his autobiography: I don't know all the certain words to word it.

Right now man you're Tom Cruisin' for a bruisin'.

DOUCHE-BAGUETTES

I think that our laws, I mean, I look at how the law originated, even from Moses, the Ten Commandments. . . . That's how all of our laws originated in the United States, period. I think that's the basis of our rule of law.

—Katherine Harris (1957–), Republican representative from Florida

I believe that mink are raised for being turned into fur coats, and if we didn't wear fur coats those little animals would never have been born. So is it better not to have been born, or to have lived for a year or two to have been turned into a fur coat? I don't know.

—Barbi Benton (1950–), American model, actress, and former girlfriend of Hugh Hefner

IT WAS GOD WHO MADE ME SO BEAUTIFUL.

IF I WEREN'T, THEN I'D BE A SCHOOL TEACHER.

—Linda Evangelista (1965–), Canadian model

FILIPINOS WANT BEAUTY. I HAVE TO LOOK BEAUTIFUL SO THAT THE POOR FILIPINOS WILL HAVE A STAR TO LOOK AT FROM THEIR SLUMS.

—Imelda Marcos (1929–), widow of Philippine president Ferdinand Marcos

I LOVE BEING ALL-NATURAL.

—Paris Hilton (1981–), American heiress

I'm not anorexic. I'm from Texas. Are there people from Texas that are anorexic? I've never heard of one. And that includes me.

—Jessica Simpson (1980–), American singer and actress

I THINK THAT *CLUELESS* WAS VERY DEEP. I THINK IT WAS DEEP IN THE WAY THAT IT WAS VERY LIGHT. I THINK LIGHTNESS HAS TO COME FROM A VERY DEEP PLACE IF IT'S TRUE LIGHTNESS.

—Alicia Silverstone (1976–), American actress and star of *Clueless*

WHY SHOULD WE HEAR ABOUT BODY BAGS AND DEATHS . . . ? IT'S NOT RELEVANT. SO WHY SHOULD I WASTE MY BEAUTIFUL MIND ON SOMETHING LIKE THAT?

—Barbara Bush (1925–), first lady of the United States

THE DOUCHEBAG HALL OF FAME:

Ann Coulter

(1961–), AMERICAN POLITICAL COMMENTATOR

The government should be spying on all Arabs, engaging in torture as a televised spectator sport, dropping daisy cutters wantonly throughout the Middle East, and sending liberals to Guantanamo.

Liberals can believe what they want to believe, but let us not flinch from identifying liberalism as the opposition party to God.

My only regret with Timothy McVeigh is he did not go to the *New York Times* building.

SO, WHERE'S THE CANNES FILM FESTIVAL BEING HELD THIS YEAR?

—Christina "Xtina" Aguilera (1980–), American pop singer

Fiction writing is great. You can make up almost anything.

—Ivana Trump (1949–), Czech-American socialite, model, and ex-wife of Donald Trump

I WOULD NOT LIVE FOREVER, BECAUSE WE SHOULD NOT LIVE FOREVER, BECAUSE IF WE WERE SUPPOSED TO LIVE FOREVER, THEN WE WOULD LIVE FOREVER, BUT WE CANNOT LIVE FOREVER, WHICH IS WHY I WOULD NOT LIVE FOREVER.

—Heather Whitestone (1973–), Miss Alabama 1994 in the Ms. Universe contest, answering the question "If you could live forever, would you, and why?"

I DON'T THINK I SHOULD BE HELD RESPONSIBLE FOR ANYTHING I DON'T KNOW ABOUT.

—Kathie Lee Gifford (1958–), American TV host, on employing sweatshop children for her Wal-Mart clothing line

AS PUTIN REARS HIS HEAD AND COMES INTO THE AIR SPACE OF THE UNITED STATES OF AMERICA, WHERE, WHERE DO THEY GO? IT'S ALASKA. IT'S JUST RIGHT OVER THE BORDER.

—Sarah Palin (1964–), Alaskan Governor and vice presidential candidate to John McCain, explaining to Katie Couric why Alaska's proximity to Russia gives her foreign policy experience

What I'm hearing which is sort of scary is that they all want to stay in Texas. Everybody is so over-whelmed by the hospitality. And so many of the people in the arena here, you know, were underprivi-leged anyway so this [chuckle] this is working very well for them.

—Barbara Bush (1925–), first lady of the United States, on the Hurricane Katrina evacuees at the Houston Astrodome in 2005

WE DON'T PAY TAXES.
ONLY THE LITTLE PEOPLE PAY TAXES.

—Leona Helmsley (1920–2007), American real estate tycoon who willed $8 billion to her pet dog

I MAKE JESSICA SIMPSON LOOK LIKE A ROCK SCIENTIST.

—Tara Reid (1975–), American actress